TO FILL AND REF

WITH ETERNITY

FAIZ AHMAD

'*The purpose of art is not, as is often assumed, to put across ideas, to propagate thoughts, to serve as an example. The aim of art is to prepare a person for death, to plough and harrow his soul, rendering it capable of turning to good.*'

-   Andrei Tarkovsky

SOFTLY

'*And if there was no death, our hand would keep looking for something..*' (Sohrab Sepehri)

Outside the window

      centuries lie buried

            beneath the constellations

A bird spreads its songs

            and the sun sets in the farthest song

Why is everyone walking into the red sky?

From the burning end of my cigarette

an anguished sigh

            rises into the streets of yesterdays

People fall off my head

            one by one

               like forgotten songs

One day I shall die

            so softly

even my chest wouldn't know

ENIGMA

I am terribly alone and

the vast sky

suddenly turned into a wingless bird

and fell and fell.

What is happening

and why do i not know things like

What happens to the leaves

         when the tree drifts into a dream?

From which direction does the night arrive

           in that distant planet?

From which window shall the hoopoe be heard?

And if there was no sorrow,

         would I be counting the bricks on each wall?

Why does no one feel the birds fading in the sunset?

Winter night

and suddenly I know

that my life is no longer

a place for laughing butterflies

THREE HAIKUS

noon; on the hillside

autumn trees had something to

feel lifeless about

from the silent mist

a train arrives and breaks

the night in two

outside the window

someone breathes from beneath

the fallen leaves

VIGNETTES

I

An old man

wipes his glasses

with a handkerchief with no corners.

He remembers in circles.

He cries in circles.

II

A day labourer stands on a

pile of red bricks.

He adds another brick in his plate

when someone shouts

'No colour matches my dinner.'

III

A man lights up a cigarette

to live once more

in the span of the cigarette.

He ashes and he ashes

to make sure

he is not dead yet.

IV

A grocer sits within

a big glass jar of himself.

He shuts his eyes

into a dream.

The sun descends down

upon his shoulders.

V

A vagabond sleeps without his stomach

on a dead footpath.

So many cars drift by.

A glass window separates him

from you.

VI

Someone passes me by

on his ant

Another man passes me by

On his ant

and another and yet another..

I follow their backs

until the ants swallow them.

SOMEWHERE

What is it that feels like

        a cold night flowing in my blood?

Outside, a hundred birds flew for the last time

I was in love

      but within whose sleep?

A few winters ago

        we were frozen in an auroral dream

Your eyes glowed

       but I was moving away

To break out of the monotony of living

       the poets died in their own hands

In a car

night moving along with the window

       me and the stars

         shall end

           somewhere

FOUR HAIKUS

agonied breaths of

the winter moon matches the

tick-tock of my clock

a dream jumps from

sea to sea in search of

my forgotten years

and someone waited

until the road was lost in

dead yellow leaves

last summer

something within me

withered

2:38 AM

In a brief, paralyzed moment,

when the footsteps faded into

the sound of footsteps.

When century-long tears sprouted

from a palm-sized palm.

When a shoulder lost itself

out of loneliness.

When your jaws choked

at the sight of a tomorrow

shrinking to fit itself away from you.

When you picked up a handkerchief,

white and painfully white,

to die in its corner.

In that brief, paralyzed moment,

night shall escape the nest of night.

Blood shall turn bloodless.

Knees shall sink at the faintest whisper

and I, with my ears pressed against

the soft chest of all that remains,

would wonder,

with infinite and unparalyzed wonder,

'How beautifully it all started!'

NIGHT CAUSES NIGHT

The night dying between the fingers

Beneath the lonely hours

        The shoulders crumble

Somewhere, a dog is chasing

        A solitary car

Familiar silence

        At the bottom of my breaths

The clouds ride on the wind's back

And the moon fades

        And fades

           Like a memory

ENDINGS ARE WITHOUT

The sun spills   outside its circumference

All the lakes of this place

                 cradle a moon in their stomachs

Ah, how the day spreads itself

                   Across the old clock

Your sea becomes a part of my feet

Beyond seasons

                 You oscillate in your imaginings

You rise in your unspoken phrases

Tulips chirp in my silvery dreams

Delicate horizons rise and fall

                 Within my chest

And suddenly

           It all ends

            Without

BEYOND

The night nibbles at my shoulders

A deer grazes my moments

        My longings

        My eternal grass

Of our embrace

         Only my arms remain

The fan spins gradual dreams

           At the feet of my gaze

My palm goes on and on

And the sides of the room weep in them

        Someone shall rise from

      Beneath the shadow of years

And fall into my arms

PROGRESSIVE DECAY

Houses standing on their rooftops

The heavy breathing of buildings

      Falls

            And crushes the leaves

The sky migrates into a brief corner of itself

In your throat

      A civilization falls

No more tears

As you behead yourself

PRIMEVAL CALL

I am alone

and someone is calling my name

from beyond the seas of the world.

My hands are weak

and the moments escape

from the edge of my fingertips.

My bed is cold

and my eyes always watch the

longest part of night on the wall.

I am sad,

sad like the pen that

travels along the white page of separation.

I talked to the people of this town.

There is no breeze that

blows over their words.

Nobody takes the shade of

the oldest palm seriously.

I saw shadows that open their wings

above every sleeping man.

There have been moments of delight too.

I met a woman in spring time,

who was so lost in comprehending the flowers,

that their colours sang hymns

right in her eyes.

I saw a poet who,

like a cloud,

was full of rain that washes the words.

I saw many children,

their hearts full of balloons

that had escaped into the winds of time.

Someone is calling me again.

I shall leave this place.

I shall sail with the waves.

I shall sail with two dreams on my lips.

The walls around the loneliness

of a fish shall break,

and the blue song of sea shall pour.

Dawn shall overtake my boat,

and lead me into the

widest expanse of myths.

The sky shall drift into my silence,

and like a bud,

I shall blossom from the ancient soil.

THREE HAIKUS

from this direction

life spreads like a green dream

in the horsc's sleep

perched mynas;

pecking at the sun with

thin yellow beaks

against an old wall

a ladder waits for the sky

to climb down

WIDE FOREHEADS

In the starless expansion

Of this century's silence,

I am contracting within

My narrow shoes

Where I walk and I walk

Not absurdly, for my heart rests on leaves,

But still as weary,

Until I feel green enough to wear them.

One needs a touch

Or a closed eye touch

Of water pool above the end of days.

It cannot be otherwise.

How many times must we die

Behind our backs?

Oh friend, without a palm sized grief

For not yourself,

Oh friend, without a hundred doves

Beneath your ribs,

Oh friend, with cemented eyeballs

And momentary shoes,

Your wish for a wide forehead

Has brought death away from you

And death close to you.

IN A HYPNOTIC JUNGLE

I am human

Naked in front of leaves

Naked, across time.

I am human

For there are stars

And in this black night

I ache human, more so.

I am the geometric silence

Between my breaths

These breaths, larger than being alive..

These breaths, watching themselves..

I am human

In my scantily leaved thirsts for a moment of sky.

I am human

In my desire, to tie the daylight to my umbilical cords.

I am human

For I know not what seems to persistently elude me.

I stare from inside my eyes,

At that stretched moment on the wall.

A faded palm where I drowned each day!

I am human

When I burst into oranges

In this basket in my hand.

How strange

And wonderfully strange,

My lamb grazing what I lived through.

I am human,

Most of all,

When I know you are, too.

ACCEPTANCE

Rain with iron hands

strangles the slender neck

of dizzy lamps.

It is cold upon the skin!

A thousand fingers

point to a thousand directions,

Rain measures my despair

with its heartless eyes.

Now, I feel black

as if I am on the lip

of disintegrating into shadows.

Rain with iron hands

is twisting the arms of

what I imagined life to be.

Sorrow is in three parts

if I divide it

with green hands.

The third part is when

I feel the closest to

being alive.

WINGED TULIPS

The night is composed

of countless windows,

each window opening

into the desert shaped

loneliness of mine.

I am dimensionless

like a sky spread across centuries.

If you ask me a strange question

I may reply with

an arc of heaven's song

in my mouth.

I am suddenly aware

of the growth of

thirsty mouths from the

surface of my skin.

This is how it is then:

I know

I became the mountain

that I wished to move.

I know

how a bird feels

when the sky is snatched

from its wings.

I know

I am made out of verses

and my fingers

are acutely aware of

this longing

to pluck a poem

from the sad eyes of a tulip.

The feeling of the vanity of the passing world kindles love in us, the only thing that triumphs over the vain and transitory, the only thing that fills live again and eternalizes it. And love, above all when it struggles against destiny, overwhelms us with the feeling of the vanity of this world of appearances and gives us a glimpse of another world, in which destiny is overcome and liberty is law.

(Miguel de Unamuno)

MOTHER

This is all I do:

I have a blue cage

which I sometimes utter.

At other times,

death is a blue cage

which opens itself in my thoughts.

At other times,

I am thinking of mother.

her hands became mother

her prayer became mother

the longer I thought.

'And to your parents, goodness'   (The Koran)

MAYBE

I am sad

because I am not.

Death fills its lungs

with the air I breathe.

A season is lurking

behind the decayed law of leaves.

I am sad

because I am not.

A train died in

the arms of its whistle.

A house is measuring itself

in homeless eyes.

I am sad

because I am not.

A tomorrow is hanging lifeless

like so many more tomorrows.

I am floating, dimly aware that

there is no sum

that shall lead me to the beginning.

COLD EXISTENCE

Tonight

if you rest your hand upon

this strange silence of mine,

you maybe reminded

of a cold stone

aching to feel the road's endless sadness

or you maybe reminded

of words that lost their

warmth as they became distant.

Tonight

all of my existence

is staring back at me

with its blank, unblinking eyes – freedom laden.

Where shall I flee?

Where shall I flee?

I, who stretched my arms

to match time,

am thirsty like an empty cup,

thirsty for clusters of violet

that grow if a window opens itself.

My soul is real,

real like those moments

when I had nothing to do.

I am cold

and imagine how cold

would the soil's cry be,

if sunlight became tired and heavy

before it could reach the earth's lips.

Tonight

I no longer wonder

at the fact that my dreams

have lost their sleeping place

as I stare at the swinging of mirrors

from my lonely bed.

Tonight

I shall turn my face away

from those offers

that promised truth in their

vague, colourless hands.

Tonight

I became a white cloud of my thoughts

I became a gap sunken in the

ambiguity of two sleeps.

Yes, I am scattered across time

and my heart is witnessing

the birth of eternal longings.

'If there was no eternal consciousness in man, if a bottomless void never satiated lay hidden beneath all – what then would life be but despair?' (Soren Kierkegaard)

A HOPEFUL FLIGHT

'Near the tree

is a garden-line greener than God's dream.

Where love is bluer than the feathers of honesty'

(Sohrab Sepehri)

My heart is full of windows

that open to the green pastures of leisure

that open to the direction of wind

that open to the transformation of shadows.

The journey to friend's home

is ripe with metaphors

behind blue doors

and remember

to not grieve

when the heart sheds its clothes

beside the pregnant lake of loneliness.

The sky may extend

a friendly hand to

a sad faced passerby

and dreams shall hatch

like eggs

in his eyes.

In this ashen room

of my small existence,

a bird on the rooftop is spreading its wings,

as gently as life in my palm,

with hope drawn from a child's breast

I shall soar above green dreams.

A LOST EVENING

A temple repeats itself

The milk years

                Have been swallowed by my trousers

And I wonder

Who would've bitten this apple

                Had I not been born?

The sound of insects

                Falls upon the ears of the sound

The tree that once grew

        Out of my knee joints

                        Is dead

Oh mother,

It's dark in here like the insides of a whale

The song that you used to sing

                Is turning white like its corpse

ISN'T THE SKY GLOOMY TODAY?

'Isn't the sky gloomy today?'

A traveller asked.

'Sky is just a metaphor

for a lover's heart'

I replied.

We have laughed a lot today.

Come, let us shed a tear

that carries the transparent

heaviness of suffering of lives.

And look at these people!

How infected they are,

with the hidden colours of sorrow.

A woman is counting the heartbeats

of a memory upon her fingers.

'Where is tomorrow?'

I asked her.

'Tomorrow is further than a

word caused by the growth

of time between two hearts.'

She replied.

I walked along the road,

the impact of sun's presence

could not illuminate memories.

People are so dazed and lost,

what is it they are trying to recall?

Is it the sad sensation of time

flowing in between their two fingers?

or is it the hymns that their

mother used to sing to keep them warm?

Past is just a way of looking

at the incoherence of this moment.

The night has dreams to offer.

Come, let us close our eyes

and search for life

in the flow of those dreams.

THE DUSTY CORNER

At the dusty corner

around which the

footsteps of life had

taken a turn,

stood a tree

between the branches of which,

a spider had built its home.

What a flimsy home!!

A sudden rush of memories

could destroy it in a moment.

The tree leaned over

the rhythmical side of sorrow.

Perhaps it had fallen in love

with the endless colour of loneliness.

And loneliness, what a beauty!

Loneliness flows in the wind

that brings a little bird to the

sad heart of the sky.

Loneliness took me to the

cypresses between two stars.

And it carried me to the

depth of a drop.

A CLOCK

A clock hung at the sadder

corner of the wall and

I noticed a memory that

had joined the tired hands

of the clock, and was going

round and round.

'Life is a routine',

mother said.

'Life is a window,

through which we stare at a dream.'

I replied.

My mind drifted into the

plain field of innocence

of my childhood.

I lay down on the grass

To feel the caress of smiles

As I watched a cluster of violets grow

next to mother's affection.

What a warm sight!!

'People talk to you a great deal about your education, but some good, sacred memory, preserved from childhood, is perhaps the best education. If a man carries many such memories with him into life, he is safe to the end of his days, and if one has only one good memory left in one's heart, even that may sometime be the means of saving us.'

(Fyodor Dostoevsky)

ABSURD FOOTSTEPS

With the big boulder of existence

upon my back, I trudged along

the meaningless side of the mountain.

and the sound of my absurd footsteps

joined the fading laughter of the sun.

I was tired.

and clouds of despair floated

across the surface of my soul.

I let the boulder fall off my back

and watched it roll down the slope.

And then it was night.

A star lit up, brighter than others.

I sat down under a tree whose branches

extended to the edge of my solitude.

The width of perception could not

contain the strange colour of life.

The heart of the mountain is pining

for a sip of Divine Light.

And the mind travelled to the greener

side of memories.

Perhaps my childhood would come

running from behind the mountain.

And my hand touched the lips of a tulip

and love overflowed.

One must always be in love.

Love, and only love can acquaint you

With the hidden colour of grief.

And only love can introduce you to the

music of eternity's heartbeat.

Love is the silent rejection to the

categorization of objects.

My eyelids could feel the gentle

weight of sleep.

And my senses were going senseless.

I closed my eyes.

A splash was heard

as the big boulder fell

into a distant dream.

HEART IS A HORIZON

A tree with

the blue sky perched in its dreams

and all the bird sounds

overflowing from its arms

can flood into you

like a comforting ray of light

that you ran after for years

and if there is

something that still makes you

want to feel not so decayed,

remember that all the leaves

that you ever touched

were simply a part of you

'Sorrow prepares you for joy. It violently sweeps everything out of your house, so that new joy can find space to enter. It shakes the yellow leaves from the bough of your heart, so that fresh, green leaves can grow in their place. It pulls up the rotten roots, so that new roots hidden beneath have room to grow. Whatever sorrow shakes from your heart, far better things will take their place.'

(Rumi)

'From the words of the poet men take what meanings please them; yet their last meaning points to Thee.'

Rabindranath Tagore

Printed in Great Britain
by Amazon